The Injury Management Challenge

By Margaret Spence

The Injury Management Challenge Published by DCRC Training Group, Inc. a Publishing Division of C. Douglas & Associates, Inc.

ISBN: 978-0-9789407-1-3

Book Website: www.WorkCompSeminars.com

Editor: Linda Alila – LindaAlila.com

Cover Designer: Daniel Barrozo – The Ink Studio ~ theInkStudio.net

C. Douglas & Associates, Inc.
P O Box 211835
West Palm Beach, Fl 33421
561-795-3036

Injury Prevention and Management
is Everyone's Business

Coming together is a beginning; keeping together is a process; working together is success.

Henry Ford

Contents

Resources Guide to Simplify Injury Management Challenges

This book is grounded in simplicity. The concepts are easy to apply.

We need you to help us create a climate in which injury management challenges become improvement opportunities.

I wrote this book because Supervisors, Managers and Team Leaders make or break the Workers' Comp process. Employers are constantly challenged to get their leadership team to understand the important role that supervisors play in the process. Companies often lack the will to have tough discussions with their supervisors and managers.

Your manager handed you this book for a reason. Please don't put it on the shelf.

You have the opportunity to make a difference in the outcome of the workers' compensation claim. I want you to step up your game, align your goals with ours, stop complaining about the system, value your employees, and lead the process. I want you to mobilize your energy and help us make extraordinary improvements in how we manage injuries and how we keep them from happening in the first place.

Really Simple Concept

If your actions **inspire others** *to dream more, learn more, do more and become more,* **you are a leader.**

John Quincy Adams

Managers, Supervisors, and Leaders:

We need you to actively participate in the Injury Management Team. Your role in the process is vital to allowing our company to succeed. We must value our employees before and after they are injured. We realize that managing workers' compensation injuries has inherent stresses, but we need you to help us by realizing that:

- The employee's injury is not a personal attack on you. (Check your Ego at the Door).

- Filling out paperwork is not an annoyance.

- Investigating accidents is vital to our prevention strategy and will allow us to document our files to prevent future litigation.

- Communication is imperative and allows us to avoid delays that increase cost.

- Our ability to control our bottom-line cost is dependent on your cooperation.

- Complaining without actionable solutions only adds to the problem.

It's not about you – it is about them, your employees. We can't continue to operate on the assumption that we will fix the employee after the injury. We have to focus keenly on what we can do to keep the employee safe every day.

We depend on you to help us create a culture of safety.

Nothing personal, but…

Workers' comp injuries are a ***symptom of our leadership failures***. Honestly, the injury could be avoided. We have an opportunity to instill safety everyday if we ask one simple question:

What are we overlooking, condoning or accepting that could lead to the employee's injury?

Starting today, we're going to stop focusing on *why stuff happened*, and start focusing on *what was done to cause it to happen*.

1 – We Need YOU

The Framework – What your participation means to our bottom line

Injuries cost real money. It is often said that unless you understand what they cost, you will never appreciate why specific choices are being made. Let's define what injuries cost.

Key Facts:

- A workplace injury takes place every six seconds, which means 96,000 each week.

- The total cost of work-related deaths and injuries was $176.9 billion.

- The largest component was not medical costs — it was wage and productivity losses ($86.8 billion).

- Medical costs $43.2 billion, and then administrative expenses were $32 billion.

- The average cost of an injury that required medical treatment was $37,000.

In 2010, the cost per worker of workplace injuries was $1,300. This means that each employee working in the United States must produce $1,300 of goods or services *just to offset the cost of workplace injuries nationally*.

Also, an estimated 60 million days of work were lost due to injuries and deaths. An additional 50 million days were lost due to injuries that occurred in past years. Put another way: injured employees stayed off work for 164,384 Years. Simple math – 60 million divided by 365 days in a year.

(From National Safety Council 2012 – Accident Facts)

If these numbers don't reaffirm that the injury is not about you but about them, I don't know what will.

The key takeaway:

- when we ask you to cooperate with helping us get injured employees back to work,

- when we enlist your help and understanding to reintegrate them back into the system, or

- when we ask you to help us create a culture of safety,

…we are asking you for a really good reason!

It is no longer sustainable for our organization to accept the inevitable cost of injuries. We have to do more to keep our cost in check while maintaining a safe work environment. **Everything starts with safety.** Results-driven safety requires leadership.

After employees are injured on the job, we need your leadership to keep them at work. This means keenly appreciating that return to work is the most viable option for our organization.

Do you understand what your participation means to our bottom line? If not, now's your time to ask, because going forward we are holding you accountable for your actions. As the Manager, Supervisor or Team Leader, we expect:

1. **Cooperation.**

2. **Keen understanding** of how important your role is in the workers' comp process.

3. **Continuous feedback** to help us eliminate safety concerns that could lead to injuries and reduce the overall cost if the employee is injured

The cost of every workers' compensation claim increases when we do not create a team of people who manage the process effectively. Delays in accessing medical treatment can double the cost of the claim. Incomplete documentation can cause us to accept claims that are clearly not work-related. **This is why we need you as an engaged participant in our workers' compensation team.**

Our utopia is to have an injury-free work environment, but we can't do it without your vigilance.

Don't be afraid to give up **the good** *to go for* **the great.**

John D. Rockefeller

2 – Leadership

Why we need YOU to lead

The number-one reason why injury management fails is that we lack the courage and leadership integrity to address what's really going on in the fiber of the organizations structure. Like any disease that's festering, symptoms rise to the top – but we often ignore the signs until it's too late to create an actionable cure.

In workers' compensation, the symptoms include:

- **Near misses:** injuries that almost happened or weren't as severe as previously thought.

- **Litigation:** the employee feels that hiring an attorney is the only recourse after the injury.

- **Employees faking injuries:** employees deciding to be less than honest about their injury or its symptoms.

- **Supervisors:** making exceptionally poor injury management decisions

- **Culture:** walking through the corporate door every day, knowing that there will be a new pile of injuries waiting on your desk.

We bury our heads in the sand, denying that leadership is at the core of our injury issues. Instead of shining a light on ourselves, we instead focus on the symptoms. We project our anger on the doctors, on the workers' comp system, or even onto the injured employee.

Do your organization a favor: *stop making excuses!*

Address injuries as a failure in leadership, then hold leaders accountable for creating sustainable solutions. **Start today.** That is the most important goal. Value your employees enough to ask them to help you meet that goal.

Safety is a Culture

We either have it or we don't. In order to prevent injuries, we must have a culture that will not overlook even the tiniest detail that could lead to an employee injury.

In every organization, the four areas of concern are:

1. **Onboarding:** What can we do to instill safety as a culture when employees join our organization?

2. **Retention:** What can we do daily to get employees to understand that safety is the only option? How do we ensure that being injury-free is our top priority?

3. **Core Competency:** How do we evaluate the employee's skill level and determine what training or resources they need to be successful and injury-free?

4. **Retention/Reintegration:** When employees return to work after an injury, how do we get them to understand that we are keeping the "W" in work? As the supervisor, it is essential that you manage, lead and support the employee's retention and reintegration back into our workforce. It may not be easy, but then again, nothing is.

To help us identify deficiencies in safety culture, we need your leadership to define strategies that will improve the four areas of concern mentioned above. **We also need you to ask two very specific questions every day:**

1. What can I do to correct any leadership deficiencies — within my work area or the organization as a whole — that will keep even one employee from getting injured today?

2. What can we sacrifice or change in our work process that will allow the employee to work safely?

Follow up by communicating your findings to everyone who can make a difference. Stop the unsafe act *now* before the employee is injured.

> *"We cannot ask employees to do volumes of work without a keen understanding of how that work is affecting them or may lead to injuries. The employee is not the root cause of the injury – the process, exposure or conditions contribute to the injury cycle."*

As a leader, we want you to address this at every meeting that you attend. Starting today, ask yourself and your team, "What have we overlooked, accepted or condoned that can lead to an employee getting injured right now?"

Speak up – you're in a no judgment zone. Remember, we can't make sustainable change without your input.

3 – Focus on the What

Instead of Asking Why, Evaluate the What

The injury that happened yesterday is never the cause of your organization's problems. It is a symptom of an internal leadership crisis.

The long-standing solution in workers' comp is to attempt to legislate and predict the **Why** – causing us to completely miss the **What**. We haven't figured out that we cannot legislate leadership. We cannot insure leadership, nor can we predict injury value *until we address leadership failures*. Every injury starts with a Human Resources decision. Accepting this means we address the root cause of the organization's deficiency.

Fixing this fixes our injury cycle.

It is our belief that when employees are injured we focus on the wrong question. We become fixated on the Why.

"Why did the employee get injured? Why did the employee stick his hand in that machine? Why won't he cooperate with our return-to-work request? Why is the claim costing so much? Why did our cost increase by double digits? Why is the system not working for us and seems to be working for the employee?"

The question we fail to ask ourselves is, "What?"

What did we overlook, accept or condone that lead to the employee's injury?

By overlooking the What, we end up creating vehicles to support our Why. Find the answer to the What, and you will never have to crunch the numbers or ask the Why.

So let me ask you again:

What did you overlook, accept or condone that lead to the employee's injury?

Here are some of the "What" questions you need to focus on:

- What causes employees to get injured?

- What causes them to have no loyalty to our organization or their job?

- What did we do in the hiring process that assured us they would be injured today?

No **worker**, *whether low-skilled and low-wage, or highly trained, should be injured, or lose his or her life for a* **paycheck**.

OSHA Director

- What value did you instill when the employee arrived at your company? What have you done to maintain the value proposition?

- What are you doing in the on-boarding process that's keeping employees from understanding the importance of safety?

- What have you done to evaluate the employee's core competency and what have you done to match the employee to the job you're asking them to do?

- What can you do to link fairness, human value and understand as you supervise our employees?

- What have you done to continually validate the safety exposure of the job you're asking the employee to do on a daily basis?

- What are you willing to invest in and give up so our employees can remain injury free every day?

I would like to add two other significant "What" questions to the list:

If employees continually hire attorneys after they are injured at your company, ask yourself the following question:

- What causes injured employees to feel that a settlement check is validation for the injustice of the injury?

If you are the HR Manager reading this book – here's a two-part question for you:

- What have you done to define what a good hire means to your internal dynamics?

- What have you done to quantify what a bad hire costs your company, in real dollars and cents?

Starting today, pledge the following:

When employees are injured at our organization we will not bury our head in the sand. We will conduct a thorough review of the injury, illness or exposure to discover ways we can prevent this from happening again. We will not stop there; we will also evaluate how our actions or inaction impacted the injury. We will not be passive "Why" questioners. We will become active participants in finding out what happened.

Take the Safety Survey in the Resources Section Now (see page 51).

***Opportunity** is missed by most people because **it is** **dressed** in overalls and looks like **work**.*

Thomas Edison

4 - Our Team

Like it or not, you are a member of our Injury Management Team.

Other members include:

- Employees
- Injured Employees
- Safety Directors
- Human Resources Managers
- Insurance Adjusters
- Treating Physician
- Ancillary Medical and Non-Medical Providers
- Nurse Case Manager
- The Lawyers (Yes, them too)
- Anyone who contributes to getting the employee to recover from their injury and return to work as a contributing member of our workforce.

Do we have members of the team who we don't like or who are unwelcomed?

Yes and No. I'm sure you're immediately thinking that the injured employee and the attorneys they hire are surely our enemy. No, not really. The real enemy is changing our process as an overreaction to the employee exercising their right to legal representation.

Our enemy is not litigation or the employee hiring an attorney. Honestly, it is the employee's right to hire an attorney; we can't stop that. It is your responsibility to respect that fact and keep doing what you are supposed to do as a Supervisor or Manager. Don't take it personally. Don't single the employee out for ridicule. Don't make the employee feel inadequate. It is your job to be a leader. Leading means that you continue to be a supervisor and advocate for keeping the employee working.

Think of your team members as participants in a marriage that has no divorce options. We have to find ways to get along, even when we disagree with the tactics employed to drive us off our game.

Check your ego at the door when employees have an injury and focus on developing a keen understanding in the following areas:

- **Developing empathy.** Try to understand how the employee's injury is affecting his or her daily life, and the ability to do his job. If you were injured on the job, what would you want your employer to do for you? Don't assume that every injured employee is a fraud, and don't assume that the employee is not in some degree of pain. As a supervisor, it is your job to manage the employee with a keen understanding of how the injury affects him or her.

- **Effectively managing the injury and the injured employee.** Ask questions, but do not share sensitive information and blend the employee's restriction with the job. We need to accommodate and monitor for compliance. It is not your job to decide if the employee is faking it—end of discussion! It is your job to provide the opportunity to work. If the employee chooses to violate that opportunity, then there is an HR policy to address that.

- **Blending Management with Policy.** Don't start enforcing rules that you haven't dusted off the shelf in years. Don't decide that you are a detective. Yes, we want you to provide us with information that can affect the outcome of the claim, but you are not Sherlock Holmes and you never will be. Match the job with the existing rules, and monitor for compliance.

- **Engagement.** Help the employee become an active participant in their recovery. This means we will not bait other employees to shame them into compliance. We will give the employee guidance on how to access medical treatment, we will help them navigate the workers' comp system, and we will advocate for their recovery.

The only place **success** *comes before* **work** *is in the dictionary.*

Vince Lombardi

5 – Communication Includes Documentation

Investigate, Document and Communicate

Paperwork is not an annoyance; it is our CYA Plan.

"If it's not written down it didn't happen" – that is the golden rule of documentation. When injuries happen here, it is your duty as the supervisor/manager to investigate, document and communicate your findings to either the HR Department or the appropriate workers' compensation claims liaison. This could include providing information to the insurance carrier.

No information is irrelevant or minute in the workers' compensation process. We want you to document because we cannot retrieve information after the fact. Documentation must happen in real-time, immediately.

As a supporting member of our injury management team, you cannot pretend that the accident didn't occur. If an employee approaches you and says, "I think I am injured," you need to stop everything and focus on the employee's complaints. It is up to you to gather facts and document the alleged injury. It is never your role to accept or deny a claim – you are a conduit of information, not the judge and jury. We pay our insurance administrator huge sums of money to make the final determination if the injury claim should be accepted or denied, but we cannot help them do their job without appropriate information.

The key steps in documenting any incident, even if there is no resulting injury, are known as the "Five W's" of an investigation. You are going to gather the *Why, What, Where, When* and *Who*. After that, we focus on the How.

An effective investigation will answer the following questions:

1. *Why* did the accident happen?

2. *What* were you doing when the incident occurred?

3. *Where* did the accident occur?

4. *When* did it happen?

5. *Who* saw it happen?

6. *How* did the accident happen as it relates to the job you were doing?

After getting the answers to the "five W's," you should then focus on the How. How did the accident happen? What sequence of events contributed to the accident?

We are looking keenly to link the injury to the work done at the time of the injury. Sometimes we are so fixated on the idea that this couldn't possibly happen here, that we fail to link the incident to the job. It is critically important that you evaluate the job and its tasks to see if the injury is plausible. As supervisors, if we are in a rush to fill in the paperwork, you will miss key information that is vital to accepting or denying the injury. Not everything that happens at work, actually happened at work. Not every injury is an injury as defined by workers' compensation. Without documentation and specifics on the accident, we are open to picking up everything as work-related.

After the employee says, "I'm Injured," you should:

1. **Compete the appropriate Notice of Injury Form.** Confirm the employee's contact information and make sure you note the correct injured body area(s). Be specific on the body areas (e.g. left vs. right upper/middle/lower back) because we don't want roving injuries that start out in one body area and end up somewhere else. *Do not drop the employee off in the office expecting someone else to do the paperwork!*

2. **Start the investigation of the injury.** Focus on the Five W's and then ask the How. If the accident occurred the way the employee is describing it to you, they should have answers to every question. If you ask the questions in the order listed above, the sequence of questions leaves no room for vague answers. Vague answers are a red flag to issues down the road.

3. **Report the claim to the insurance carrier if that is your role.** If not, provide as much documentation as you can to the appropriate workers' compensation coordinator in your organization.

4. **Send the employee to the doctor or call 911.** Either way, if the employee is seriously injured all bets are off. The paperwork is secondary to the employee's well-being.

5. **Welcome your employee's return post-injury.** When the employee returns to your department after the accident, do everything you can to make them feel that they are still a valued member of your team.

6. **Document and communicate anything relevant to the injury.** including time off that is not related to the accident claim, late arrivals, non-compliance and problems the employee may be having as they try to navigate the workers comp system.

Your role is to investigate and validate the accident, be an advocate for the employee, monitor for compliance with safety rules, document and communicate to avoid legal trouble, and consistently supervise the employee until they are released to full duty work.

Review: Accident Investigations & the 5 W's + H in the Resource Section – (see pages 54).

6 – Injury Management as a Customer Service Process

As I stated before, workers' comp injuries are not about you. If you were injured on the job, you would expect the process to work for you, so why not allow the process to work for the injured worker?

Here's what you need to know about the process, in simplistic and non-legalese language:

- The employee is entitled to *statutory benefits*, meaning there is a law that gives them this benefit even if we don't agree with the law. (Get over it.) These benefits include:

    ○ **Medical Treatment:** Employees are entitled to medical treatment until the doctor releases them to full duty or says they are as good as they are going to get. This opens up a lot of disputes, but this is not something you need to deal with.

    ○ **Lost Wages:** If the employee cannot come to work and get a paycheck, they are entitled to be paid for time lost from work based on the state-mandated percentage. If they are released to return to work with restrictions, and we send them home because their injury is an annoyance, *they are entitled to get paid for lost wages!* This is why we offer a job to employees who are released to return to work with restrictions.

○ **Impairment Rating:** if the injury caused permanent damage, the employee is entitled to a scheduled benefit for the injury/impairment assigned to their condition.

There are lots of variations to everything I mentioned. Still, as a Supervisor, Manager or Team Leader, these are the key elements that you need to know.

Every organization has the potential to spend millions of dollars on-boarding new employees. On average, it costs between 3 and 6 months of the new employee's salary to recruit her, take her through the hiring process, and acclimate her to our work environment. It takes even more money to train the employee to get to full productive capacity. Because of this cost, we have to look at the employee's value to the organization after they have an injury. **We have invested thousands in the employee up to the point of the injury. Do we just let that investment walk out the door? Prudent organizations don't let that happen.**

The most important thing in **communication** *is* **hearing** *what isn't said.*

Peter Drucker

We can take the following approach:

It is our philosophy that injured employees should be valued. We will make every effort to get them back to work within their restriction, unless bringing them back to work would cause a business hardship. If we can't bring them back to work right away, we will continue to make every attempt to keep them working if the doctor provides us with reasonable "restrictions."

Or we can take the following approach:

Every employee that works for us who has an injury is a loser and they don't belong here. Next! Find me a new employee to fill this guy or gal's spot.

What message do you think that sends to the morale within our organization? Would you want to be discarded because you temporarily can't perform at 100%?

Fact: 80% of all injuries are legitimate, and the employee has potentially sustained a life-altering condition. Less than 20% of injuries start out as fraudulent. However, **poor customer service, poor management and reluctant supervisors** cause good employees to become our worst nightmare.

Before you make the decision to take the accident personally and apply undue pressure to the injured employee, stop and ask yourself: *would I want this to happen to me?*

7 – Ability, Never Disability

Supervisors, We Need You to Help Us Manage our Talent – Even if they have an injury!

Pause and Reflect:

Think about the last employee who filed a workers' compensation claim at our company. After the injury, did the employee return to work successfully? If yes, then we saw the employee's ability to continue working and we did not focus on what the employee couldn't do.

Now think about an employee whom we sent home without offering a light-duty job. Do you see their ability to work, or do you see a disabled brand?

Everything is grounded in perception. If we perceive disability, then the employee will be disabled. If we perceive ability, the employee will work to his or her ability. We want you to see the employee's ability and stop focusing on inability.

We will no longer ask doctors to tell us if the employee is disabled. Instead, we will ask doctors to tell us what the employee can do. We must frame the discussion that we have with injured employees around their ability. Instead of saying, "Your doctor told us that you couldn't lift more than 25 pounds," we should instead say, "You are assigned to this work area, and there is no lifting that will prevent you from working."

One of the complaints I hear from supervisors is, "I tried to bring the employee back to work in my department but they complained the whole time they were here, so in frustration we sent them home." **There will always be employees who manipulate the system. If you think about this honestly, this employee was probably already a problem before they had the injury.** The injury only served as a catalyst to magnify their already bad behavior. There isn't a lot we can do about people who manipulate the system—that is human nature. When employees manipulate the workers' comp system, we have to trust that our insurance company will utilize your state's laws to manage the process effectively. As I said previously, 80 percent of all injuries are legitimate and the employee returns to work successfully. Unfortunately, the 20 percent that don't cooperate get all of the attention.

Key steps to re-introduce your employees to work:

- **Contact the employee.** Let him or her know that you have a position available that is within the restrictions.

Treat **Your People** as You Would Want **Your Customers** to Be Treated.

Lee Cockrell –
Former EVP of Walt Disney World

- **Sit the employee down before they return to the work area and review the exact job requirements.** Go over the tasks you are assigning to them and make sure they understand exactly what they can and cannot do.

- **Go to the work area and make sure the employee understands the job and the accommodation.** Point out the tasks they are allowed to do and the ones they should avoid until they are released to full duty work.

- **Reassure the employee** that you are there to address any concerns they may have about doing their job successfully.

- **Explain that this assignment is temporary.** As they progress medically, additional duties will be added to their day.

- **Step back from the situation and recognize that you are not there to babysit the employee.** Your purpose is to guide, support and direct by actively supervising the employee to prevent overexertion or a new accident.

- **Address concerns that the employee has with empathy, and provide a solution.** Do this even if you think the employee is playing games. Remember, you need to stay in the game; don't allow yourself to be played by the game.

- **Track all medical appointments.** Ask the employee how they are doing after the appointment, and document any issues that arise. If the employee is referred for additional testing or has a specialty referral, make sure you relay that information to the insurance adjuster or your internal workers' compensation coordinator. We are here to advocate for and facilitate immediate access to medical treatment. Delays in accessing medical treatment can double our overall claims cost.

- **Document and communicate any issues that you observe about the employee.** Keep accurate records of the employee's work schedule, especially when they are on restricted or light duty. Document any missed days from work, disciplinary actions or counseling sessions due to non-compliance. *Do not harass the employee.* You are not here to suddenly step up your supervision because you are on a war path.

- **Ask for help.** If you have questions about the process, don't be afraid to ask someone who had more knowledge about workers' compensation like your HR Director or your workers compensation adjuster.

Your role as the supervisor or manager is to advocate ability and squelch the disability mindset.

Management is doing things right; **leadership** is doing the right things.

Peter Drucker

8 – Fundamental Value Proposition

Selling Success – When we win, we need to take credit for winning.

Workers' compensation is not a game, so please don't apply the analogy of winning to a game mindset. Instead, **we win when three fundamental things happen:**

1. The culture within our organization is keenly focused on injury prevention.

2. We create an environment where every employee is valued, even if they have an injury.

3. We systematically create a management structure that has a singular goal of rooting out failures in our leadership and finding ways to produce without having unproductive injuries.

We win when injured employees are able to go out for medical treatment and return to work in a productive capacity. We win when we keep the definition of work in the forefront of the workers' compensation process.

Ask yourself this key question every day: **Did my employees feel valued by the organization before the injury? Do they still feel valued after the injury?**

Employee engagement is a key factor in managing injuries. Employees are either engaged in their treatment and recovery process, or they are disengaged and ready to derail the process. It's up to YOU, the supervisor/manager, to keep the employee engaged when they come back into your workforce.

We must help injured employees see that they can be innovative, creative and add value to the organization's bottom line. Otherwise, we are headed for the litigation zone the minute they disengage. The best ambassador for a disgruntled employee is someone who can say, "When I got injured, they took really good care of me. I don't understand why you are making this out to be such a big deal. The company cares about us, so stop the disruption and go back to work." Do you think you could find an injured employee in your ranks who was willing to advocate the company's position on injury management? If not, then we need to change how we value injured employees. They are our brand advocates, or they are the fuel that others use to damage our corporate image.

You can help us become a more successful injury management team if you:

1. **Immediately assess** the injury and the injury exposure

2. **Create a corrective action strategy** to keep the injury from happening again

3. **Advocate for the injured employee** to make sure they are getting adequate and immediate medical treatment

4. **Identify Ability without focusing on Disability.** Help us find productive work for injured employees as they transition back into the workforce.

5. **Treat the employee with respect** and don't take their actions personally. Help them transition back to work successfully and spread the message that this is what we expect when you are injured.

6. **Document everything** that happens so if we need the information we are not draining the swamp in your brain to find it. No one said injury management was going to be easy but we are dependent on you to make sure we stay out of legal hot water. Your actions or inactions have consequences across every fiber of our structure.

I'm **not concerned** *with your liking or disliking me... All I ask is that you* **respect me** *as a* **human** *being.*

Jackie Robinson

Lessons Learned

The 8 Simple Reasons why we need you to stop complaining about the workers' comp system and start helping us create a proactive injury prevention and injury management team are:

Lesson 1:   **Injuries cost our organization real money.** We can no longer accept injuries as the inevitable cost of doing business. We are depending on you to help us create an injury-free work environment.

Lesson 2:   **It takes leadership to address deficiencies within our organization.** We need you to step up and lead your team so they understand that we will make safety a cultural shift in our workforce. Reward safe acts and discipline non-compliance. Be a leader and help us indemnify our deficiencies by creating actionable solutions.

Lesson 3:   **Don't blame the employee solely for the accident.** Instead of going in circles asking why the accident happened, ask what caused it to happen so that you can create change. We can only get better if you are willing to ask the tough questions.

Lesson 4:   **You are a valued contributor to our success.** You are a member of our injury prevention and injury management team. If we are dysfunctional, everyone suffers.

Lesson 5:   **Documentation is not a chore—it is a requirement.** Write it down, communicate in real-time, and be consistent with your supervision.

Lesson 6:   **Injured employees are your customers when they enter the workers' comp system.** It is up to us to treat them with respect, even if we don't agree with the tactics they deploy. We are here to make good things happen even when bad things occur.

Lesson 7:   **Inability is Out; Ability is In.** We will no longer communicate in terms of employee "inability." We will only communicate in "ability." This is what you can do, and I am here to help you do it.

Lesson 8:   **You are here to help us win the injury management process.** It's not a game but a life-changing, essential, business survival strategy. We need you to help us sell success to our skeptical team members. Engage your employees in the injury prevention process, and engage injured employees in their recovery.

Really Simple Concept – now go out and lead the change. We need you to lead our team.

Leadership is **solving problems**. *The day soldiers stop bringing you their problems is the day you have stopped* **leading** *them. They have either lost* **confidence** *that you can* **help** *or conclude you do not* **care**. *Either case is a failure of* **leadership**.

Colin Powell

Resources Guide to Simplify
Injury Management Challenges

- Safety Survey

- Risk Identification Questions

- Accident Investigation 101: The Five W's and the How

- SWOT Analysis Worksheet

- 7 Essential Steps to Get Injured Employees Back to Work

- Glossary of Terms

Safety Survey

Your opinion counts! Lend your voice to our safety goals.

What are the three positive programs or safety initiatives at our company?

Name the two basic safety requirements that are essential in your department or work area.

What is the one safety policy that every employee follows diligently or 100%?

What's great about safety at our company?

Who thinks safety is not important?

Do employees feel that they are in a safe work environment every day?

Why do you think employees get injured in your department or work area?

What one thing would you do to improve our safety culture today?

Risk Identification Questions

Safety Equals Real Solutions for Your Least and Worst Exposures

For each position that has repeat injuries, evaluate the following areas:

Job Description:
- What are we asking the employee to do?

Job Tasks:
- What are the specific steps to complete the job?

Inherent Dangers:
- What are the inherent dangers or risks associated with the job or task?

Safety Mandate:
- What is the safety mandate for that job or task?

Controls:
- What safety controls can you put in place to ensure that the employee will be safe?

Communication:

- How will you communicate the safety requirement to the employee?

Compliance:

- What procedure will you put in place to make sure employees are complaint with the established safety rules?

Remember: we must be willing to Rinse and Repeat. Continuously ask these questions until you assess the risk and eliminate/minimize the exposure.

Accident Investigations 101: The Five W's and the How

- Accident investigation is a key component of your job as a manager or supervisor.

- You demonstrate your leadership abilities by completing a thorough investigation of each accident to enable our organization to remain injury-free.

- The investigation is here to highlight ways to improve our process and to increase our safety vigilance.

The steps:

First Ask – What:
- What were you doing when you got injured?

Next Ask – Where:
- Where were you when you got injured?

Then Ask – When:
- When did you have the injury?

Then Ask – Who:
- Who saw the accident?

Finally Ask – Why:
- Why did you get injured?

Pause, Evaluate, and Continue to the How.

Ask the How:
- How did you get injured? Tell me how this happened again?

Your next step:

Evaluate if the job or job task could cause this type of injury. Go to the work area and compare the account of the accident with the description of the job task. Does it match? If not, why not?

Document your findings and discuss it with your insurance carrier.

Then, ask the "Internal What": What are we doing to do to make sure this incident doesn't happen again?

SWOT Analysis Worksheet

Honesty Gauge – To enact change, we must be willing to ask tough questions, challenge the norm, and create actionable solutions — today. Answer honestly and without blinders.

Strengths: What are the positive things about the safety process or procedure in your department?

Weaknesses: What are the clearly defined weaknesses to establishing safety in your work area?

Opportunities: What are the Great reasons why safety is important and why you can make immediate improvements to prevent the next injury? Who can you recruit (must be a line employee) to help you develop or improve the safety program?

Threats: What specific things stand in the way of getting safety established within the culture of your Department or work area? Who dislikes the safety program? Who is the most vocal critic? Who thinks safety is just a waste of time?

Next Steps

What are you going to do to turn Threats into Opportunities, and Weaknesses into Strengths?

Tribe of Believers

How do you plan to win over the naysayers and build a winning team?

Sacrifice

What work process are we willing to give up or drastically change so that employees remain safe every day?

7 Essential Steps to Get Injured Employees Back to Work

- Identify tasks that can be grouped together to accommodate the injured employee's restrictions. Focus on matching the employee's ability to do the job versus focusing on what they cannot do.

- Send a copy of the proposed modified-duty job description to the treating physician, and ask him or her to approve the position. You are asking the physician to acknowledge that the employee can complete the tasks based on the restrictions imposed. This avoids the "I'm in too much pain to do this job" scenario.

- Notify the injured employee by phone and in writing that you can accommodate their restriction. Ask them to come back to work.

- When the employee returns to work, review the position and inform the employee that the treating physician confirmed their ability to perform the modified tasks.

- Educate all supervisors so they can effectively manage the injured employee within the restriction. This insures that you adhere to the light-duty restriction.

- Communicate the job offer to your insurance carrier. Document any non-compliance and communicate any issues to your workers compensation team. Remember you are an advocate for the employee as well as the company. If the employee is having a problem accessing medical care it is imperative that we find a way to help them resolve that issue promptly.

- Continue to monitor the employee until they are released to work full-duty or until they are at Maximum Medical Improvement.

Glossary of Terms

Temporary Total Disability (TTD)
The period of disability during which the injured employee is totally disabled and unable to perform any work.

Temporary Partial Disability (TPD)
Employees are eligible for benefits if the doctor has given the employee a medical release to return to work and the employer is unable to offer the employee any work within their restriction.

Permanent Total Disability (PTD)
The injured employee is permanently disabled and will never return to gainful employment.

Maximum Medical Improvement (MMI)
The date the employee is released by all treating physicians, and the employee is considered done with treatment. The injured employee is as good as he or she is going to get.

Impairment Rating (IIB/IB)

A special one-time benefit paid to the injured employee because they sustained a permanent impairment due to the injury. Payment is made despite the employee's ability to work.

Return to Work (RTW), also called Stay at Work (SAW)

A program designed to bring injured employees back to work as soon as they are released to return to work. The goal of the program is to offer injured employees meaningful, productive work within their restriction.

Always bear in mind that **your own resolution** *to succeed is* **more important** *than any other.*

Abraham Lincoln

We are here to show our employees that we value them despite the injury.

This is not a win or lose concept – it is a win/win proposition.

But if you fail to lead and we get it wrong, we all lose.

Acknowledgements

Special thanks to my incredible publishing team. Linda Alila my editor (LindaAlila.com) and Daniel Barrozo Creative Director and Senior Editor at the Ink Studio (theInkStudio.net) in Long Beach California for putting me on the schedule and delivering a great cover and interior design. Simple but beautiful.

This book is dedicated to all the Supervisors and Managers who diligently manage workers compensation injuries every day.

To my valued clients who encouraged me to write a book that spoke directly to Supervisors and Managers, and to all the readers of my blog, the WorkersCompGazette.com who leave wonderful comments that spurred me to action – Thank you.

About the Author

Margaret Spence is the President/ CEO of Douglas Claims & Risk Consultants, Inc. and WorkCompSeminars.com. The core foundation of her company is a commitment to helping employers implement proactive workers compensation and integrated disability management policies, that retains or returns ill, injured and disabled employees to the workforce. Margaret is an expert at showing companies how to navigate the often-complex workers' compensation system and create policies that link HR best practices with prudent injury management strategies.

Margaret is the author of *From Workers Comp Claimant to Valued Employee*. Her new book, *The HR Manager's Survival Guide to Workers Compensation Injury Management*, will be published this summer. She has written extensively for many business publications on return to work implementation, worksite wellness, post-disability inclusion and she is a national speaker on workers compensation. Her blog, The Workers' Comp Gazette (**http://WorkersCompGazette.com**), was awarded the 2010 - Top 25 Workers Compensation Blog by LexisNexis. Margaret was a three-term member of Society for Human Resource Management's Special Expertise Panel on Employee Health, Safety & Security, and she is the two-term VP of Professional Development for the Greater Miami SHRM Chapter. She was recently appointed to the HR Disciplines Panel and serves on the board of the Workers Compensation Institute.

You can reach Margaret at

www.MargaretSpence.com or email her at **BookInfo@MargaretSpence.com** or call her at **561-795-3036**

One Last Thing:

If you got anything out of this book, please order a copy for your management team. We cannot afford to have Managers and Supervisors disconnect from the workers' compensation process. They have to sit at the table and be a contributing member of the injury prevention and management team.

The Injury Management Challenge is available for bulk purchase through www.WorkCompSeminars.com/Challenge

Margaret's other book, *From Workers Comp Claimant to Valued Employee*, can also be found at the website.

To purchase additional copies of the book or training materials please visit us at:

store.workcompseminars.com
or call 561-795-3036

Notes:

Notes:

Notes: